For Alf, Rosa and Blod
Nita Clarke

for Anna, with love
Phil

First published in 1984 by Writers and Readers Publishing Cooperative Society Ltd,
144 Camden High Street London NW1 0NE England

Text copyright © 1984 Nita Clarke
Illustrations copyright © 1984 Phil Evans

ISBN 0 86316 078 6

Typeset by Lithosphere Printing Cooperative Ltd 203-205 Pentonville Road London N1
Printed and bound in Great Britain by Oxford University Press

LONDON FOR BEGINNERS

A political history of London

by Nita Clarke
and Phil Evans

INTRODUCTION

SINCE THE end of the Second World War power in Britain has been so centralised around Whitehall and the government of the day that the major British cities have not had the recognition and influence of their opposite numbers in North America and Western Europe.

London has suffered from this problem more than most because the media in London report national events, with little interest in the municipal affairs of the city that shelters them.

Those who have been amazed at the current media obsession with the GLC should talk with the residents of New York, Paris, San Francisco or Amsterdam, to discover that this level of interest should be normal for any city of the size and economic clout of London.

What is unusual is that city politics in Britain has been such a backwater for so long. Elsewhere, it is accepted that the political leaders of major cities are just a step away from national political leadership, yet in Britain the emergence of the new municipal socialism is condemned as much for its presumption in daring to say "no, prime minister" as for its alleged "overspending".

This excellent guide to London puts today's problems in their historical context. The lessons of the English Revolution and Civil War were not lost on successive governments. London was a base for progressive forces and a danger to the establishment of the day. This is why London was the last British city to be allowed to elect its own council. And no sooner had the old London County Council been created than Conservative governments began to talk of its abolition.

Nothing that has happened in the these last three years is new. The Liberal progressive administration of 1889-1907 fought for cheap fares, police accountability, council housing and trade union rights.

It was vilified by government and press in exactly the same terms as the present GLC administration.

At one point the chairman of the LCC was a notorious Mr Benn (grandfather of Tony) who was defeated in a parliamentary by-election at Bermondsey after a vicious campaign by a newspaper called the "Sun". ·

During the next year we shall learn the result of the struggle to keep the GLC working for London. The fact that the outcome of that struggle is still in doubt – although the Government has a majority of 140 in the House of Commons – is an indication of the vitality of the city and its people.

That vitality is the subject of this book. In the long term there can be no doubt as to who will be the victors in this new battle for London.

Ken Livingstone
September 1984

LONDON
FOR BEGINNERS

> Come, we will walk.
> I pray you, let us satisfy our eyes
> With the memorials and the things
>   of fame
> That do renown this city.

WILLIAM SHAKESPEARE.

LONDON BEFORE THE ROMANS

As everyone knows London is a Roman creation. When the Empire conquered Britain, it was clear that the Thames River was of strategic importance. With its outlet to the North Sea it was one of the traditional invasion routes and its valley was a vital route inland.

Veni, vidi, pluvit.*

LONDINIUM

* I came, I saw, it rained.

GREATER LONDINIUM COUNCIL COUNTY HALL (OR 'FORUM')

There were already small British village settlements along its course, but the Romans set up their major trading centre at a good site for more permanent settlement, where the gravel beds gave a firm foundation, and the tidal flow suited Roman ships. This first town, around the area where the Tower of London now stands was undefended, a trading post for the import of wine, foodstuffs, military equipment and other necessities for a military occupation.

7

It soon fell to the first major British uprising against the invaders, and was sacked by **Boudicca** and the Iceni tribes in AD 61, when the Roman Governor **Suetonius Paulinus** decided that, since the settlement was undefended, discretion was the better part of valour and withdrew his troops.

BOUDICCA

The rebuilt settlement, with its three-mile Roman wall, became the administrative, financial and commercial centre of the province. By the end of the third century almost 60,000 people lived, worked, and traded within its boundaries. Across the river, where Southwark now stands, a suburb developed.

SOUTHWARK
WELCOMES
CAREFUL
DRIVERS

...he City was known as a pleasant place to live.
...he state buildings and the homes of the rich
...ed Roman styles, built of brick, stone and tile.

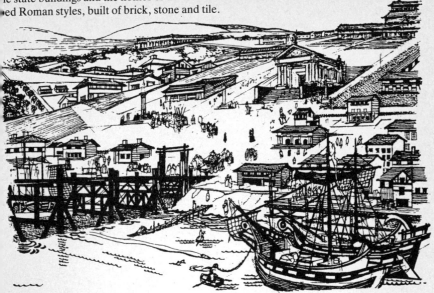

...he labourers and peasants had to be
...ntent with huts and wooden houses.
...was also an exceedingly prosperous
...wn for the wealthy, as the remains
...f Roman luxury goods show; so do
...e remains of industries including brick
...lds, potteries, masons yards, joiners
...ops and mills, cobblers, and foundries.

...arms outside the walls supplied fresh food. Unpolluted water was still available from the
...hames, the Fleet and Walbrook streams.

The Roman City declined with the Empire. By 457 refugees from Saxon and other raids on Britain were streaming into the town from all over South-East England. Life in the City kept going, however. Londoners already had the reputation as an independent lot. Under the Romans it was neither a tribal centre nor a *colonia* (where ex-legionnaires were settled as a reserve of veterans in time of trouble), and under early Saxon times it stood outside the organisation and legal system of the country as a whole.

In the seventh century, for instance, Londoners threw out a Bishop sent by **St Augustine** himself to convert the City to Christianity and reverted to their old religion.

The City was sacked by the Danes in 851, but Good **King Alfred** – while rather dubious bout Londoners' jealously-held demands for independence – secured it as a base and drove ut the Danes.

He then redeveloped the town inside the old walls, giving grants of land to loyalists.

I always burn the cakes. That's why they call me **Alfred the Grate!**

Even the Danes were better than the Tories!

TYPICAL MALE CHAUVINIST DANE OF THIS PERIOD

The City was once again an unrivalled commercial and trading centre with enclaves of foreign merchants; wine merchants from Rouen, merchants from Germany, and Danish families settled in the area (one group under their leader **Osgod Clapa** giving their name to Clapham).

London.

The southern suburbs had already established a more relaxed reputation: Sudwerke became a royal borough well known as a centre for fun and disorder, "a wild disorderly haunt of rakes, drunkerds and whores" as one historian put it.

EDWARD THE CONFESSOR

I muft confeff – thefe bramblef are very fcratchy !

The centre of Westminster came into existence when **Edward the Confessor** resettled his court there around the new Minister of St Peters on Thornea, or Isle of Brambles, one of several islands – Chelsea (Isle of Shingle), Bermondsey (Bermond's Isle) and Battersea (Peter's Isle) – in the marshy ground upstream of the City's western wall.

St Peter in Westminster

WILLIAM the CONQUEROR.

THE TOWER OF LONDON

William the Conqueror didn't much trust the inhabitants of Lunduntown. Straight after his coronation he moved from Westminster to Barking, until 'certain strongholds were made in the town against the fickleness of the vast and fierce populace'. One of these strongholds built to keep Londoners under the Norman thumb – the White Tower – still stands, marking the eastern boundary of the wall.

– and that's for King Harold, Norman!

DONK!

ARMS OF THE CITY OF WESTMINSTER

Neither the Normans or their successors ever succeeded in controlling London entirely and were never sure of its loyalty. Although grants of land inside the walls were continually made to royal supporters, most of the land and nearly all the trade, commerce and manufacturing remained in independent hands. The independence of the City was confirmed by Royal Charters, while the organisation of the traders, merchants and manufacturers into powerful guilds and trade associations meant that commercial life was tied up in a series of tight closed shops which came to control most of the economic life of the country.

"Turn again, Whittington — Lord Mayor of Great London".

They were powerful enemies, as **King John** discovered when London sided with the Barons against the royal power, which could unleash powerful discontents – as the City discovered when the apprentices opened the gate of London to **Wat Tyler** during the Peasants' Revolt in 1381.

KING JOHN

MAGNA CARTA

Maybe I should bring in some **anti-trade union legislation!**

THE PEASANTS' REVOLT

NO MORE TAXES

DEATH TO THATCHER

FREE THE SERFS

LONDON

Tyler himself was killed by the City Mayor.

Thanks for killing Tyler, Mr Mayor – now can you go and kill Livingstone!

Although there remained open spaces such as marshy Moorfields, where the adventurous skated over the frozen marshes during the winter, the City was becoming a crowded and a dangerous place to live. It was filthy, with refuse, offal, ordure and industrial waste tipped into the streets. The water supply became polluted as streams such as Walbrook became clogged up. Walbrook was described as a mile long public latrine.

Houndsditch (part of the ditch built outside the walls) got its name from the large number of dead dogs to be seen floating in it.

There was of course no town planning, and
centuries of higgledy-piggledy development,
much of it in timber construction, overlay
the Roman streets. Despite royal orders for
all future building to be in stone and tiles
no-one took any notice. Fire and disease
were the major threats: the Black Death in
1348-9 – the most virulent outbreak of the
ever-present plague – carried off an
estimated two-thirds of the City. 30,000
corpses alone were disposed of in vast pits
dug – and consecrated by the Bishop of
London – in Smithfield and other areas.

Scab Mite

Fires were an everyday hazard, despite the orders which required each City ward to provide
equipment such as poles, hooks, chains and ropes for the instant demolition of a burning
house.

By the twelfth century 75,000 people crowded within the walls. Splendid noblemen's and merchants' houses grew up amidst the hovels and shanty towns of the poor, the workers and the vagrants.

There were other dangers to life and limb; visitors constantly complained of the appalling smells, of the signs hanging outside each shop or workplace which protruded into the streets and either fell on the heads of the unwary during a strong wind, or knocked riders off their horses.

Londoners were a byword for unruliness and violence and for having a good time while they were at it – much of it directed against 'foreigners' – which meant anybody seen as a threat to established trades. Street battles were common between apprentices and competing tradesmen. In 1222, after a London wrestling team beat their Westminster opponents, the return match turned into a pitched battle, and was followed by Londoners taking revenge by attacking the Abbey and throwing stones at the Abbot.

Unlucky thirteen...

Thirteen apprentices were executed in the 1530s for taking part in "Evil May Day" riots – sparked off by the authorities' ban on City apprentices going out of doors on the eve of May Day because of the bad behaviour they had displayed towards passers-by in the street during Easter Week.

The retinues of noblemen were considered by all to be the worst trouble makers, swaggering through the streets and picking fights with all and sundry.

I'm bored, Percy.

I know – let's go and smash up Caxton's printing press!

William Caxton, England's first printer, working at Westminster

21

Nevertheless amid the violence, squalor and disease, the economic power of the City merchants, manufacturers and financiers thrived. They controlled the City through the corporation and mayorality, established at the end of the twelfth century – but they didn't directly control the Government. Westminster, well outside the walls and still separated by fields from the City, had become the administrative centre for the Kingdom and the home of the Royal Courts of Law. The separateness was symbolised when **Henry V**, on his triumphal return from Agincourt, was invited on a victory tour of the City, and ceremonially presented with London's keys.

Here are the keys to the City, Henry – pop them back through the letter-box when you go!

Most parts of the City and even streets were associated with particular trades: coal importers at Sea Coal Lane; fish traders at Fish Street Hill; German merchants at the Steelyard.

Southwark kept up its reputation as Fun City, outside the control of the City government. (The prostitutes by this time became known as 'Winchester geese' because the **Bishop of Winchester** owned so many of the brothels.)

Get your **nuns** gear on girls- the Bishop's here!

By 1600 this unplanned development meant that almost 200,000 people lived in, and around, the City. The lack of City government, the stranglehold of the new capitalists, often at loggerheads with the encroaching nobility, began to lead to complaints at the unrestricted growth of the City, the increasing industrial pollution, the hazardous water supply, the growing poverty of the unemployed, the rising crime rate, the vagabonds and the highwaymen, the 'beggars and other loose persons swarming about the City'.

Let's go and throw stones at the Bishop!

Theatres developed to complement the pleasure gardens; cockpits; bear-dancing; the bull-baiting rings. As well as Southwark and Westminster other satellite settlements became recognisable, like Lambeth, where the **Archbishop of Canterbury** had his Palace, and St Giles, Holborn, Whitechapel and Wapping, the lawyers' courts and temples around Grays Inn and Lincolns Inn, the Middle and Inner Temple, and the dockyard towns at Deptford and Woolwich.

ut the City government was unwilling and incapable of putting matters to rights. The
ruggle in the seventeenth century to supply clean water to Londoners shows the strength of
e vested interests able to wreck the plans of the more public spirited. Apart from minimal
mping operations from London Bridge and Queen Hythe, London's water came from
sterns all over the City, never adequate for domestic and industrial needs.

Left: Domestic
need.

dmund Colthurst had the bright idea of tapping springs in Hertfordshire and Middlesex
d digging a canal to take the water to a reservoir in the north of London. The Mayor and
ldermen and bankers refused to help. Even when one of their number, Hugh Middleton,
ok over the scheme they soon pulled out because of rising costs. Progress was slow, as
ndowners, through whose property the canal passed, refused even generous compensation.

27

James I

None of your piped sludge!

Only when the scheme secured the support of **King James I**, who apparently saw the need to bring pure water to 'those poore people enforced to use foul and unwholesome water which breedeth great infections', was it finally completed, ten years after inception. Even then, resistance to piped water was strong among householders. Their fears were fed by water carriers fearing for their jobs, who spread the rumour that the piped water was fatal: 'fresh and fair river water – none of your piped sludge'. Vandals sabotaged the canals and pipes, enterprising builders let sewers into it, and thieves stole the taps.

LONDON WATER CARRIER

O it's dabbling in the dew that makes the milkmaids fair!

OLD SONG

28

The City's response to the growing problems of sprawl was to try and prohibit building. In 1580 a proclamation prohibited any new house building within three miles of any London gate where no former house was known to have existed within living memory. It had little effect, as a further stream of regulations for the next hundred years showed. Royal building proceeded unchecked. Others evaded the regulations through bribes or determination: one builder erected a high fence round a field in Chancery Lane where he claimed to be keeping rabbits; in fact he built a row of squalid tenements. Land speculation was rife, houses jerry-built and prices and rents exhorbitant.

As a result, development outside the three mile limit continued apace. A whole series of Royal and noble estate developments sprang up: Leicester Square; St Martin's Lane, and – most notably – Covent Garden. The latter was designed by **Inigo Jones** under the patronage of **Francis Russell the Earl of Bedford** (and now restored by the GLC to something approaching its original conception).

Typical – we do all the work and Inigo Jones gets all the credit!

HARRIS's LIST
OF
Covent-Garden Ladies:
OR
MAN OF PLEASURE's
KALENDAR,
FOR THE YEAR 1773.
CONTAINING
An exact Defcription of the moft celebrated Ladies of Pleafure who frequent COVENT-GARDEN, and other parts of this Metropolis.

THE SECOND EDITION.

LONDON.

LEFT: Inigo Jones at Covent Garden discussing his original conception

I resolve to live of my own – without Parliament !

CHARLES I 1641

RIGHT: A CATHOLIC CROSS IS PULLED DOWN IN CHEAPSIDE

The question of control over the City came to a head during the Civil War and short-lived Commonwealth. To no-one's surprise, London sided with Parliament. The famous five members of Parliament sought refuge in the City during **Charles the First's** attempted coup in 1642 and the King was sent packing. Cries of 'Privilege of Parliament' were heard when he entered the city to get them back.

WHITE HALL

ABOVE : CHARLES IS EXECUTED AT WHITEHALL, 1649.

Most merchants and bankers welcomed the stability they felt sure the Restoration in 1660 would bring. Two 'Acts of God' lay around the corner that would bring the greatest devastation the City had ever experienced. Both were directly traceable to conditions within the City – the maze of alleys and courts, crumbling hovels and rotting tenements, where thousands of families lived in appalling squalor, on the breadline, side-by-side with the grandeur of the Royal Exchange, the merchants' offices and the nobles' estates.

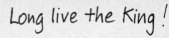

In 1665 the bubonic plague, carried by rats and infected fleas, swept London, killing at least 20,000 people. The following year on Sunday 1st September a fire started in a baker's premises in Pudding Lane, close to the River.

The flames spread, helped by the dry timber caused by a dry summer: the riverside, with its stores of combustible goods, was soon ablaze.

By Monday night Thames Street had been destroyed and the fire was approaching Cheapside in the North, burning down the Royal Exchange on its way; St Paul's and the Guildhall burned on Tuesday and the fire approached the Temple. The conflagration was helped when the Lord Mayor refused to order the wholesale pulling down of houses in its path for fear of compensation claims. By Tuesday night the fire had destroyed thirteen thousand houses and 44 of the City Companies' Halls. Almost a quarter of a million people were homeless.

was such a common occurrence
at the Lord Mayor showed
first no concern.

Pish – a woman
might pisse it
out!

I wish they'd
hurry up
with the
rebuilding –
we pigeons
haven't got
anything
to sit on!

The City authorities were
determined to rebuild as
quickly as possible on the
ruins before refugees
settled in the suburbs,
outside the jurisdiction of
the Companies. **Charles
II**, on the other hand,
wanted to rebuild on a
planned basis, to enable
the new London to
outshine model towns
like Paris, then going up
on the Continent. The
overall planning ideal did
not succeed, because of
the competing interests of
those involved, the high
cost of borrowing and the
difficulties in tracing
original owners and
tenants. Both the Crown
and the City appointed
rival City Commissioners
to control the re-building
plans. Negotiations
between Crown and City
and other interested
parties were long and
protracted.

Many plans were submitted. In the event, rebuilding under the Rebuilding Act followed the lines of the old City for the most part, although construction was generally of better quality. At least the open sewer that was the Fleet River was replaced by a canal – although this was soon vandalised as a rubbish dump. After a drunken butcher got stuck in the mud and froze to death in the 1760s it was finally bricked over.

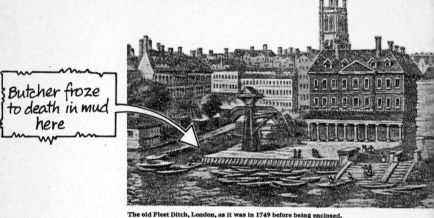

The old Fleet Ditch, London, as it was in 1749 before being enclosed.

Much of the reconstruction was slow – **St Paul's** was not finished until 1710. By this time a workman on the site had become a byword for slowness. Today, the outlines of **Christopher Wren's** grand plans can be seen only in the city churches.

Now you've finished that, lads, you can start work on the Thames Barrier!

The aldermen's fear of loss of control were realised. The new suburbs, particularly in the north, where drainage problems caused by the heavy clay soil were finally being solved, grew apace: Highgate, Hampstead, Hornsey. To the west of the City vast noble estates around Bloomsbury, Knightsbridge and the Haymarket grew up, and the royal enclosure around St James's Park led to widespread development north of Pall Mall – so called after the alley where Charles practised the ball game *palla a maglio*.

One noble, the **Duke of Buckingham** insisted on every one of his names being commemorated in the new streets on his estate: as a result we now have George, Villiers, Duke, and Buckingham streets, as well as Of Alley, latterly retitled York Place.

37

DR SAMUEL JOHNSON

When a man is tired of London he is tired of life; for there is in London all that life can afford.

Sweet Thames, run softly, till I end my Song.

EDMUND SPENSER

This is a London particular - a fog...

CHARLES DICKENS

I have seen the Mississippi. That is muddy water. I have seen the St Lawrence. That is crystal water. But the Thames is liquid history.

JOHN BURNS. DOCKERS LEADER 1880s

By the nineteenth century, London, the City and the suburbs was a teeming metropolis, of savage contrasts between rich and the poor. It was a place of largely unplanned and haphazard development, a dangerous place where the rich feared the mob, but one with many entertainments, and where hundreds of subcultures, from workers' organisations to vagabonds and thieves' societies flourished. Visitors found it as easy to find entertainment as to have their money stolen. Others were impressed with the fine buildings. Beneath the glamour were slums and tenements, grinding poverty and child labour, workhouses, prisons and gin houses.

A horse bus.

MONMOUTH STREET

vercrowding remained the main feature of life. In a single nine bedroomed house in
italfields in the 1880s there lived sixty three people sharing nine beds. Privies were
mmonly used as sleeping places by the homeless poor. Average life expectancy was about
. Only one child in three survived to the age of five. Smallpox and enteric fever were rife; in
84 over 14,000 died from cholera in London. London was honeycombed with 300,000
sspits, or cess lakes; in many areas the water supply was non-existent, or limited to a few
urs' supply a week from a communal standpipe; roads were rudimentary, paving usually
known, street lighting completely inadequate, education unavailable for the vast majority
the capital's children.

ASYLUM FOR THE HOUSELESS POOR, CRIPPLEGATE

41

Behind the showpiece buildings was urban chaos. London effectively had no government at all.

Good fing too! Govingments never did nuffink for nobody! *

* Misguided but understandable attitude of London's lumpen proletariat

Don't call us 'lumpen', you posh snobs!

Author and artists' note: Sorry.

is ironic that the most powerful oligarchy of e City had its origins in one of the earliest emocratic' or popular assemblies in Britain the Saxon folk moot.

e guilds and livery
mpanies, with their original benevolent
ciety functions and their trade regulations
hich benefited consumer and member
ike, metamorphosised into the reactionary
tes which came to dominate economic life
Britain.

At the same time the City oligarchy system proved immensely adaptable, encompassing the growing capitalist and financial class, with its vast funds derived from property, investment, trade and manufacture.

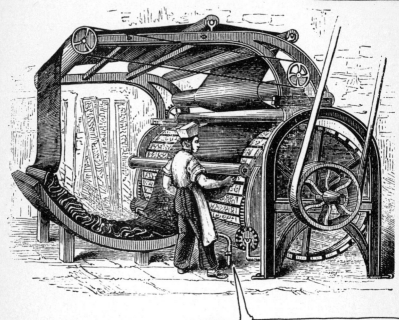

The working class cannot simply lay hold of the ready-made state machinery and wield it for its own purposes

KARL MARX

Because of the geographical concentration of its power in the ancient heart of London no attempts were made to extend the City's territorial boundaries. Instead a haphazard system of parish vestries developed over time as the capital spread. By the nineteenth century the City was the undisputed citadel of wealth and influence and regarded itself as the voice of the capital. The liverymen of the Companies of the City of London with the aldermen of the Corporation formed the Court of the Common Hall; selected the Lord Mayor and the sheriffs and other officers exercising judicial and administrative duties within the City of London. Outside the walls the mass of London with a population eight times as large had a system of government equivalent in scope and efficiency to that of a number of scattered rural parishes.

The annual parish vestry meeting allowed inhabitants qualified to vote to have some control over how their rates were spent and to elect the local constable, the surveyor to look after the roads and the overseer of the poor.

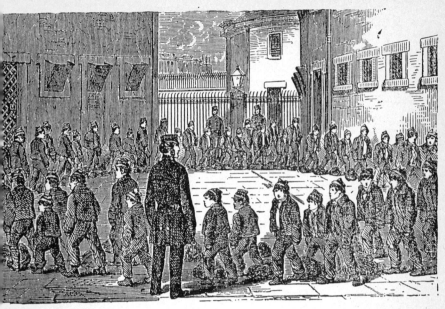

BOYS EXERCISING AT TOTHILL FIELDS PRISON

Other parts of London had only a select vestry in which decision making was confined to a few: the opportunities for corruption and pocket lining from the rates were enormous and well-known particularly under this restricted system: highways were neglected and unpaved, the destitute were ignored and crime was rife. The poorest areas did not even have this pretence at local government.

They wouldn't let me go to the vestry because I can't afford a vest!

A PICKPOCKET IN CUSTODY

45

Outside London the **1832 Reform Act** and the **1835 Municipal Corporation Act** had gradually revolutionised local government; in particular enabling the overspill areas outside original city centres to be brought within municipal administration. In London, added to the City's determination to retain control was the suspicion of central government that any extension of metropolitan government would give a voice to the dispossessed and add strength to the already powerful voice of the City. Thus all the arguments in the late nineteenth century about city-wide government have echoes in the current battle over the fate of the GLC.

I suppose this is what they mean by an **overspill area**!

There were voices raised for reform. The 1837 Royal Commission on Municipal Corporations wanted the reforms in the rest of the country to apply to London:

'We are unable to discover any circumstance justifying the distinction of a small area within the municipal boundary from the rest, except the fact that it is, and long has been, so distinguished'.

at all attempts at reform were piecemeal and fiercely resisted. Following numerous public outcries and investigations into the inadequate water supply, drainage, sewage and refuse disposal services for example, an Act consolidated the administration of sewers – except in the City – then controlled by no less than 1,065 commissioners of sewers. But the new body of twelve commissioners was ineffective; no less than six Commissions were appointed in as many years without any of them being able to secure the much needed improvements because of inadequate powers.

Above: a drop of London's water.

Cholera and typhoid found their way even into the Royal Household –

I don't feel very well, Victoria...

Oh Albert – I hope you haven't caught typhoid!

(But he had. He died from it in 1861.)

and the stink from the Thames as it passed Parliament was so bad that it sometimes forced the Honourable Members out of the Chamber, even when the bars weren't open.

I say – what's that pong?

It's Gladstone again

No, it's the rotten river!

Somebody should do something about it!

By the 1850s, the situation was out of control. There were in existence no less than 250 local Acts setting up various local boards and commissions, and 10,000 commissioners served on a hotch-potch of lighting commissions, directorates of the poor, and turnpike boards. Gross corruption led to thousands of pamphlets and meetings, where outraged ratepayers demanded reform. But many boards purposely appointed nobles and MPs to ensure reforms were blocked.

Said a Marylebone vestryman in 1830:

We always make a point of having as many noblemen and Members of Parliament as we can get hold of!

Just like a modern multinational!

When ratepayers did put forward bills to remedy abuses, commissioners intent on continuing to line their pockets from the rates bribed and lobbied Parliament to get them defeated. The pressure for reform got so strong that the Riot Act had to be read at some vestry meetings where ratepayers tried beyond endurance attempted to oust corrupt commissioners.

Above: annoyed ratepayers.

49

The road system in London was a national scandal. The **Strand Union**, for example divided its eleven miles of streets among seven paving boards each with its staff of clerks, collectors, surveyors and other officers – among them a tailor and a law stationer. Between the Strand and Temple Bar, a matter of little more than a thousand yards, the street was divided into seven paving boards. In St Pancras it cost the ratepayers £5,000 a mile to repair the roads.

When reform did finally come it represented a fatal compromise between competing interests. Under the **Metropolitan Management Act** of 1855 – a Private Member's Bill introduced by **Sir Benjamin Hall** – the City remained untouched. The parish vestries also remained as the basic units of administration but the smaller ones were grouped into fifteen districts administered by district boards. These boards together with the larger vestries became responsible for electing a central body – the **Metropolitan Board of Works**.

CITY
OF
LONDON
KEEP
ORF

You keep your vestries and we'll keep our investments.

Its remit was limited: "the better management of the metropolis in respect of the sewerage and drainage and the paving, cleansing lighting and improvements thereof". Only over these limited functions was coherent control envisaged, but as pressure for further improvements grew other functions were gradually added: inspection of gas supply, provision of an effective London fire service, providing parks and open spaces, slum clearance, and raising a poor rate.

THE PAWNBROKER'S SHOP

Following a deliberate policy of weakening the Board by the old tactic of divide and rule, the government created further bodies for other functions: the **Metropolitan Asylums Board**, the **Port of London Sanitary Authority**, and the **London School Board** as a result of the 1870 **Education Act**.

A DAME SCHOOL

Despite its weak powers and criticism from vested interests the Board had some achievements. Within ten years it had created an 82 mile sewer system with outflows outside the urban area. Open sewers were filled in.

THE GIN-SHOP

Several major new thoroughfares were built, including Victoria Street, Charing Cross Road and Shaftesbury Avenue; the north side of the Thames was embanked; ten of the Thames bridges were freed from tolls. Parks were developed – including Hampstead Heath and Clapham Common – and some of the worst slums were cleared.

But the continuing power of the vestries was the Board's Achilles heel. Most of them ignored their new powers. Refuse was left in the streets. Powers to set up libraries, public baths and washhouses and street sweepers were ignored by 'vested interests in filth and dirt' who controlled many of the vestries.

In particular the new medical officers had a hard time. The medical officer for St James's, Westminster, had his salary reduced by £50 to £150 when his vestrymen discovered he was taking his job seriously. And because these vestries elected the Board of Works, there was no direct public influence to counteract their dead hand.

Oh – and by the way, Doctor – because you're doing your job so well the vestrymen have decided to reduce your salary!

When constabulary duty's to be done, A policeman's lot is not a happy one!

The City, too, continuously hindered further reform. For example, London's police force remained divided between the metropolitan and City forces.

Reform measures in 1858, 1863, 1868 and 1869, 1870 and 1875 were successfully resisted by the Corporation. The public outcry at their scandalous methods employed in resisting the 1884 **Harcourt Bill** provoked a select committee investigation.

The Corporation had a lot to lose: the livery companies alone owned property worth £5 million, and their income was over £500,000 a year. To beat off the Bill they spent enormous sums in bribery; they hired gangs of bullies to break up meetings of the **Municipal Reform League** which was leading the campaign for reform, and they set up a bogus **Ratepayers Protection League** to campaign against the Bill.

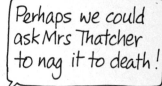

Public pressure, however, came to a head when an inquiry into the Board showed it was involved in corrupt land speculation and other scandalous practices. The Tory Government seized the opportunity of the 1888 **Local Government Act** to usher in a further bodged reform – the **London County Council**.

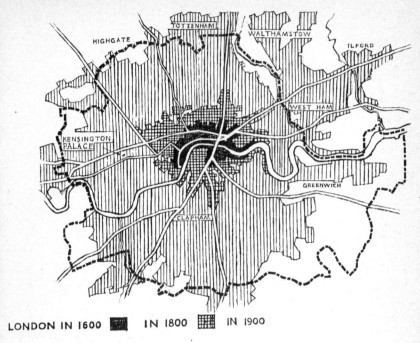

LONDON IN 1600 ◼ IN 1800 ▦ IN 1900

▥ LCC BOUNDARY 1888

In its day the LCC was world famous. Under the **Webbs** and later **Herbert Morrison**, it became synonymous with municipal socialism – "gas and water socialism" – and middle-class reforming zeal.

NEW

(*Mr. Punch's Design for a Grand*

"THE OLD ORDER CHANG

NDON.
llegorical-Almaniacal Picture for 1889.)
NG PLACE TO NEW."—TENNYSON.

Its beginnings were not auspicious. Under the 1888 Act the vestries and district boards remained intact as did the boards running the asylums, the police, the schools, water conservancy, and the Boards of Guardians.

The City retained its exclusive rights and privileges. Strengthening the county councils surrounding London made any widening of the municipal boundary impossible, making slum clearance and drainage needlessly complicated. London's boundaries remained those of the ancient districts which compiled the old **Bills of Mortality**, giving warning of the approach of the plague.

For the socialist and radical movement it was lucky that the birth of the LCC coincided with the increasing belief by the working class in the possibility of political power through the ballot box, following the succession of **Reform Acts** that had widened the franchise (the latest being in 1885). The 'new model' trade unions, largely craft-based, sought respectability and means to influence those in power, although by the 1890s general unions were recruiting the unskilled in increasing numbers

← USED BANDAGES FOR SCABS

Non-union member.

Union member.

TEA OPERATIVES & GENERAL LABOURERS
ASSOCIATION
A Registered Protective Union for General Labourers.
ALL GENERAL & DOCK LABOURERS JOIN at ONCE
and Defend the Rights of Manhood in a Practical
and direct manner.
CONTRIBUTIONS 2ᵈ WEEKLY. ENTRANCE FEE 1ˢ
(Payable in 12 weeks)

NOTICE ADVERTISING A NEW
GENERAL UNION AT THE LONDON
DOCKS.

But the reforming LCC made a powerful impact on public opinion. It frightened the Tories. In 1894, the Prime Minister, **Lord Salisbury**, turned the full force of Tory invective against the Council.

We must not be shy of using all our political power and machinery for the purpose of importing sound principles into the government of London

Lord Salisbury

"The Council", he fulminated, was "the place where collectivist and socialist experiments are tried, and where a new revolutionary spirit finds its instruments and collects its arms."

Ah - but there would certainly be a revolution **without** the L.C.C.!

UNEMPLOYED WORKERS RIOT IN ST JAMES STREET, 1886

62

The **Fabian Society** epitomised these trends: in the LCC
idney and **Beatrice Webb** and others found their
erfect vehicle. Their epoch-making tract or manifesto
acts for Londoners set out a programme of social
if gradual – reform of social conditions through
e LCC.

The Fabian line found an echo in the diverse Liberals and other reformers elected onto the fi
Council. Taking the label 'progressives' were leaders of the Municipal Reform League such a
J B F Firth, **Sir John Lubbock** and **John Benn**, and socialist **John Burns**.

JOHN BURNS SPEAKING TO STRIKING DOCKERS ON TOWER HILL

Opposing them were the Conservative 'moderates'
whose first priority was to limit the role of the Council,
and second, to keep rates down.

Below: Conservative
"moderates" protesting
about the rates.

GAS

By 1892 the progressives
stood on a programme of
municipal ownership of
the public utilities in
London – gas, water,
transport and electricity.

WATER

TRANSPORT

ELECTRICITY

People call this
"Gas and Water
Socialism" –
presumably because
the socialists gas
a lot before they
water down
their politics!

Among the Labour leaders who played a role in the early LCC, **Sidney Webb's** role was notable. He retired from his post in the Colonial Office in 1892 to work full-time to establish a secondary and further education system for London. He guided the LCC for many years.

PUNCH, OR THE LONDON CHARIVARI.—JANUARY 19, 1889.

THE "GRAND TRANSFORMATION"!!

Every step the LCC took was obstructed by vested interests: slum landlords; factory owners who ignored the **Factory Acts** and deprived children of education; public utility companies. To challenge the parasitical contractors, the LCC insisted on a fair wage clause in all its contracts. When the contractors raised their prices the Council set up a direct works department.

What does "Direct Works Department" mean, Philpott?

It means we don't (hic!) have to be ragged-trousered philanthropists any more, Barrington!

But there were defeats. The private water companies, despite annual efforts to secure a Parliamentary Act forcing them to improve services or be municipalised, remained in private hands despite public inquiries. Commission after Commission recommended municipal ownership. Whole areas were forced to rely on communal standpipes where water flowed for a few hours a day – at the same time as water rates rose dramatically.

Periodic epidemics were traced directly to the polluted water supply. The Fire Service complained constantly of inadequate water supplies for fire fighting. The Government's solution? The creation of a separate **Metropolitan Water Board**. Massive compensation was paid to the water companies. It was still being paid for out of water rates in 1945.

Tram services were equally chaotic, with fourteen companies owning and operating 107 miles of services, with no co-ordination. A journey across London involved frequent changes with long walks in between, and fares were high. The LCC began to acquire operators' leases when these ran out; the Conservative minority filibustered council meetings to prevent the vote going through.

In another historical echo of today's debates, the **Metropolitan Boroughs** were set up in 1899 as alternative centres of power, deliberately to curb the power of the LCC. There would be no co-ordination with the LCC, said **Arthur Balfour**, because –

Co-ordination with the LCC would inevitably drag these councils into the political vortex in which the LCC appears to flourish

Balfour: Tory Prime Minister 1902–1905

In the 1907 LCC elections, the scare tactics paid off. The Tories – now called the **Municipal Reformers** – won control of the Council and set about undoing as many of the progressives' achievements as possible. Not only did they see their class interests as holding down spending on services and limiting the LCC's role – many of them were closely tied to the slum landlords, private companies and monopolies, which had a stranglehold over London

SLUM LANDLORDS

PRIVATE COMPANIES

MONOPOLIES

TORIES

he same time, the political face of London was changing. The **London Labour Party** was
nally set up in July 1914.

spite the rampant jingoism of the early war years the party soon found its feet – and by 1919 ·
t confident enough to fight the LCC elections independently of the progressives, on a
inifesto of municipal ownership of all public services, including transport, food and fuel.
om 15 councillors in 1919 the Party's representative had shot up to 35 elected councillors
d four aldermen by 1925. It became the official opposition.

During the war years and the 1920s the LCC Tories carried out the bare minimum possible in improvements of housing, education, public health and public assistance. This was in contrast to councils like Poplar, in London's East End which challenged the Government head on.

Poplar was a poor borough with a rateable value of only £1 million (Westminster's was £7 million)

It had enormous problems: bad housing; poverty; unemployment. 44,000 people were on outdoor relief, compared with 400 in Hampstead.

The councillors decided that unemployment was a national problem and should be tackled nationally. They argued for a rate Rates Equalisation Fund by which rich boroughs would subsidise poor ones.

Meanwhile, the Council set about helping Poplar. New houses and 'Baths' were built. Electricity supplies were improved.

LEFT: COUNCILLOR JULIA SCORR SPEAKING JUST BEFORE GOING TO PRISON

A minimum wage for all council employees gave women equal pay. Higher rates of relief were paid than anywhere in the country.

The government refused to provide the necessary funds. The Poplar Council decided to go on a rate strike.

Councillors refused to levy rates for central bodies like the LCC and the police!

There was massive local support for this move—from street traders, trade unions and tenants' organisations.

The London Labour Party, led by Herbert Morrison, issued circulars condemning Poplar Council's actions as illegal and irresponsible.

In June 1921 the exasperated LCC took Poplar Council to court. The Court duly decided that the councillors were liable for the levies and should be imprisoned if they didn't pay. The councillors still refused.

A huge march accompanied the 5 women and 24 men to prison. At Brixton gaol the councillors asked to see the warders' union cards.

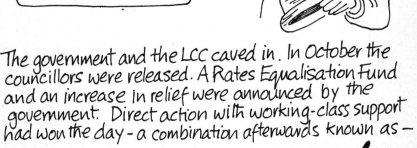

I made speeches from my prison window to huge crowds, who sang the 'Red Flag'. Other councils threatened to follow our lead.

The government and the LCC caved in. In October the councillors were released. A Rates Equalisation Fund and an increase in relief were announced by the government. Direct action with working-class support had won the day - a combination afterwards known as —

POPLARISM!

The key battle in the next few years was over London's transport. Apart from the municipal tramways, all other transport in London was concentrated in the hands of a combine which had Government backing. The combine set out to smash the LCC's trams, by running omnibuses on parallel routes at lower fares. By 1927 their sympathisers in the ruling Tory group were proposing selling off the tram services to the combine, giving it a total monopoly over the entire transport network.

There once was a man who said, 'Damn!
It is borne in upon me I am
   An engine that moves
      In predestinate grooves,
I'm not even a bus, I'm a tram.'

The scheme was only scuppered because by 1929 a Labour government was in power and **Herbert Morrison**, the Labour Leader of the LCC, was the Minister of Transport. Under his 1931 **London Passenger Transport Act** public transport in the Greater London area eventually passed from private hands to a public corporation – the **London Transport Passenger Board**.

HERBERT MORRISON

Why is publicly-owned transport better, Dad?

Well, everybody **has** to use transport, so us public should own it, son. It's like public houses!

If one factor above all others discredited the Tories in the eyes of Londoners, it was their vicious and inhuman application of **Public Assistance**. The 'economy cuts' in public assistance and councils' welfare services were imposed in 1930 and 1931, as part of the Labour Government's and National Government's futile efforts to deflate its way out of the gathering economic crisis. Massive cuts in public expenditure were the order of the day. In 1931 the Tory majority cut three quarters of a million pounds from the budget; capital spending was cut by half. The rules governing payment of public assistance were ruthlessly applied and payments pared to the bone to individuals and families – at a time when the numbers of unemployed were rocketing.

Why do tramps exist at all? Curiously, few people know that a tramp takes to the road not because he likes it, but because there happens to be a law compelling him to do so. A destitute man can get relief at casual wards... for only one night; he is automatically kept moving.

GEORGE ORWELL: 'DOWN AND OUT IN PARIS AND LONDON'

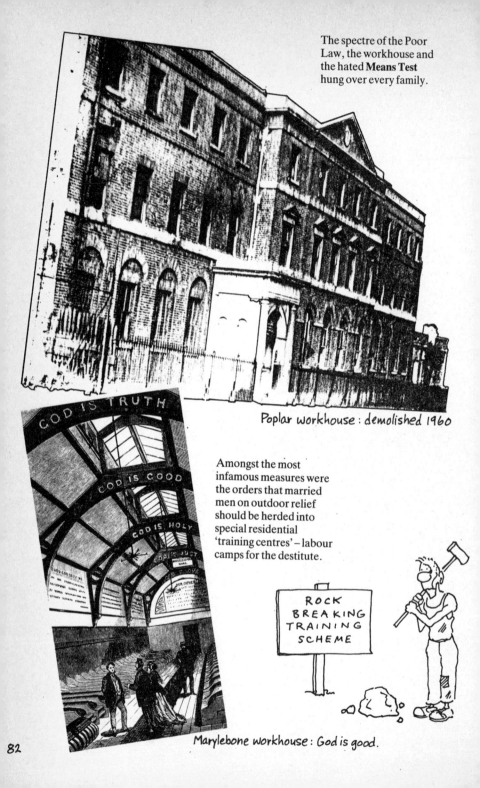

The spectre of the Poor Law, the workhouse and the hated **Means Test** hung over every family.

Poplar workhouse: demolished 1960

Amongst the most infamous measures were the orders that married men on outdoor relief should be herded into special residential 'training centres' – labour camps for the destitute.

GOD IS TRUTH
GOD IS GOOD
GOD IS HOLY

ROCK
BREAKING
TRAINING
SCHEME

Marylebone workhouse: God is good.

Such measures had the effect of depressing the economy further by reducing the demand for goods and services. The Labour group – as today – demanded a programme of increased spending particularly on capital works – denounced in exactly today's terms as 'financial lunacy' by the Tories and the Treasury. The Tories paid the price for this dismal record. In the 1934 LCC elections, Labour returned 69 councillors; with the additional aldermanic seats, Labour had a majority of 16, 80 seats to the Tories' 64. They were to keep control of the LCC until it was abolished in 1964/5.

The socialist millenium did not come, of course, as a result. The forces arrayed against the Council remained enormously powerful. As outer London expanded, the outer boroughs with their Conservative majorities and the County Councils always saw it as a priority to keep the socialist LCC at bay – and to keep the people of inner London as far away as possible. Nor were the LCC's powers adequate: scales of relief for public assistance, for example, were set by Government.

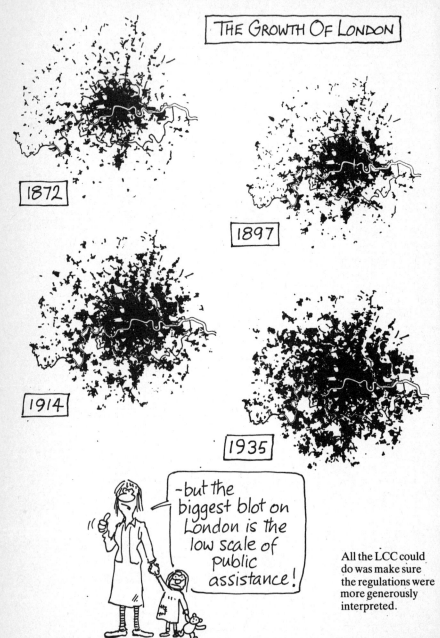

THE GROWTH OF LONDON

1872

1897

1914

1935

– but the biggest blot on London is the low scale of public assistance!

All the LCC could do was make sure the regulations were more generously interpreted.

Board of Education still set the number of teachers in Council schools, and the LCC could not abolish fees in secondary schools. Land and housing remained overwhelmingly in private hands; the LCC had to fight every inch of the way to use its compulsory purchase powers to attack the problems of slum clearance and council housing, and to create the Green Belt.

The Government retained the upper hand. It distributed grants and it alone could pass the necessary legislation to allow the LCC to get on with the job. The Conservatives in the 1930s subjected the LCC to a continuous scrutiny and control it did not apply to other councils. The rate equalisation mechanism within the LCC remained unfair.

What's rate equalisation, Cyril?

Good question, George—

Theoretically, it's the system by which the richer London areas in the LCC which can afford to charge higher rates—

—help to subsidise poorer parts of the city which would otherwise have to charge very high rates—

—to support their hard-pressed social services.

Talking of which, can you lend me a pound?

The City, the richest square mile in the world, managed its own finances. In 1938 the City Corporation spent over £9,000 in banquets and receptions alone – the equivalent of a threepenny rate in the borough of Stepney.

Providing decent homes for Londoners was the greatest challenge facing the Labour LCC. By the 1930s London's population was expanding at over 80,000 a year as more families from the depressed areas flocked to the capital.

London's boom in the new industries meant a crying need for homes for the workers – at the same time as the LCC struggled with clearing the inner city slums and overcrowded conditions that were turning large areas into new slums. As a result land values in London soared, and rents climbed. Vast new areas became urbanised overnight, with little in the way of social amenities or facilities.

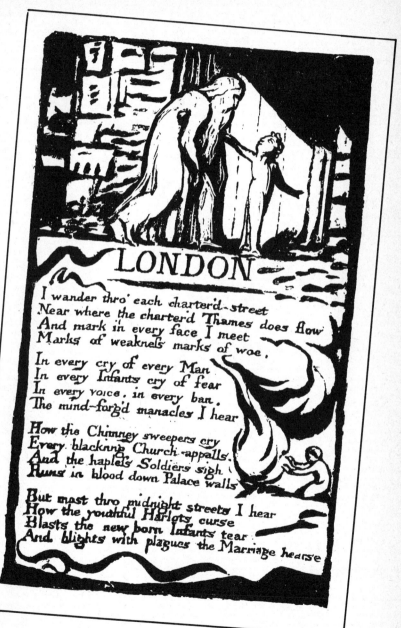

LONDON

I wander thro' each charter'd street
Near where the charter'd Thames does flow
And mark in every face I meet
Marks of weakness marks of woe.

In every cry of every Man
In every Infants cry of fear
In every voice, in every ban,
The mind-forg'd manacles I hear

How the Chimney sweepers cry
Every blackning Church appalls,
And the hapless Soldiers sigh
Runs in blood down Palace walls

But most thro midnight streets I hear
How the youthful Harlots curse
Blasts the new born Infants tear
And blights with plagues the Marriage hearse

WILLIAM BLAKE

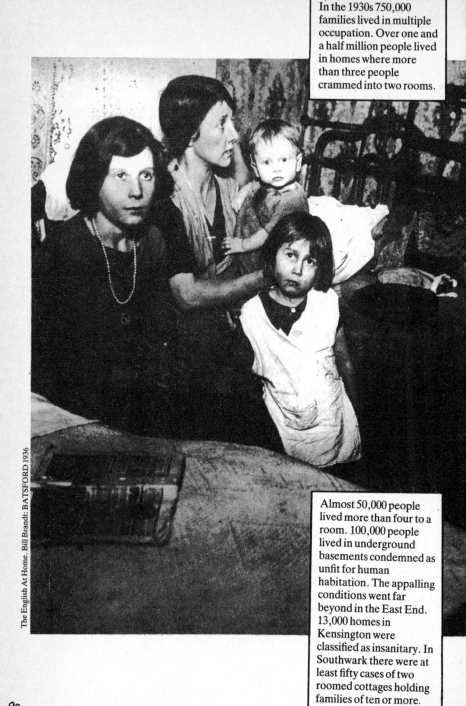

In the 1930s 750,000 families lived in multiple occupation. Over one and a half million people lived in homes where more than three people crammed into two rooms.

Almost 50,000 people lived more than four to a room. 100,000 people lived in underground basements condemned as unfit for human habitation. The appalling conditions went far beyond in the East End. 13,000 homes in Kensington were classified as insanitary. In Southwark there were at least fifty cases of two roomed cottages holding families of ten or more.

INFANT MORTALITY

TUBERCULOSIS

BRONCHITIS

PNEUMONIA

The infant mortality rate, and rate of death particularly from diseases such as tuberculosis, pneumonia and bronchitis increased in proportion to the rate of overcrowding in the area. 48,000 Londoners died each year as a direct result of appalling housing conditions.

BACK STREET ABORTION

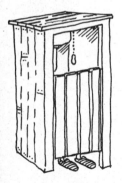
TYPHOID

MALNUTRITION

ALCOHOLISM

The English At Home. Bill Brandt: BATSFORD 1936

The Tories had concentrated on developing a few cottage estates outside the LCC area, but the rents were far too high for slum dwellers. The fares to work alone placed these outside the reach of those in most need. Between 1919 and 1924 the Tories built 375 'homes fit for heroes'. Between 1924 and 1927 they promised an extra 20,000 homes; fewer than 12,000 were built; only 118 were built between 1930 and 1934. It took 25 years to clear one slum housing 1,800 people in Bethnal Green, which was condemned as early as 1904.

The labyrinthine procedures which the Council had to pass through before a single brick could be laid were awesome. Compulsory purchase orders (where the Council acquired the properties itself) or clearance orders (where the owners retained the properties but were required to demolish and rebuild) involved initial reports, submission to the Ministry and public inquiries.

Get lost Bolshevik! Come back when you've got more papers!

The slum landlords fought every step of the way. The stakes were high and profits enormous. One 17-room house in South London, for example, was let to twelve families numbering 72 people, at rents ranging from 16 shillings to £1 8s a week. Landlords' claims for compensation were astronomical – and each contested case had to be referred to lengthy arbitration.

Even when a scheme was agreed, the people living in the area had to be placed somewhere while redevelopment was taking place, near to their places of work. Rehousing and slum clearance became a series of interlocking moves as small areas of improvements were made, people moved in and their old houses subsequently rebuilt so that more families could move in and so on... by 1938 the Labour LCC had rehoused 83,000 slum dwellers and demolished over 12,500 slum houses in over 400 acres. Altogether 30,000 new homes were built with accommodation for over 125,000 people.

Rehousing slum dwellers outside the old areas did not pass unnoticed. One of the most unpleasant whispering campaigns, stirred up by the sensational stories in the press, tried to stop the spread of 'slum minds, slum habits and slum diseases' outside the East End, with 'overspill' boroughs mounting campaigns against the new tenants. "We don't want them in our area!" was the cry.

The other major areas where the LCC set a pioneering example were in public assistance and in London's health service. Even in the 1930s the scanty provision of public assistance for the unemployed and the destitute – cut still further by fierce national expenditure cuts – was still stuck in the humiliating and degrading ethos of the Poor Law and the workhouse. Until the 1920s provision of poor relief was by local boards of Guardians.

The workhouses, into which the poor and destitute were crammed, became a symbol of all that was wrong with Britain. Families were broken up, husbands and wives separated, the elderly were cut off from their former lives and children taken away from their parents.

Workhouse conditions were deliberately made as bleak and degrading as possible. Although they were financed by a city-wide poor rate, the provision of 'outdoor relief' had to be made from local rates – the financial consequences of which were responsible for the Poplar revolt. Not until the burden on the ramshackle system had become intolerable by the late twenties with the rise in unemployment and destitution did the government concede that reorganisation was required – twenty years after the 1909 **Poor Law Royal Commission** had first called for a unified London-wide poor law administration.

The LCC's declared priorities were to make the payment system reflect individual needs and to humanise the administration of relief. The huge general workhouses, where everyone – children and pensioners, able bodied and disabled, sick or healthy – requiring relief had been traditionally dumped, were broken up. In their place the Council diversified welfare provisions to establish special homes, nursery schools, training centres and hospitals where individuals could receive the specialised care and support they might require.

Within three months of taking office the new administration increased the numbers receiving relief by 11,000. By 1935, an average of over 105,000 people were receiving some form of paid benefit a week.

The degrading system of giving food tickets was phased out in favour of cash payments; by 1935 only 5% of relief was provided by payment in kind, compared to 25% under the Tories. The public assistance committees were purged of reactionary Tories. The Council decided to drop the term 'public assistance'. Instead the social security and welfare services would be known as social welfare.

It is true that the system remained paternalistic and bureaucratic. Relief rates set by government stayed low, and Labour councillors were at pains to point out that the idea of relief was not endless doling out of public funds enabling the idle to live off the state. But, on the whole, the kinder – if firm – way the system came to be administered was a revelation – and a revolution. The welfare revolution was a major factor in the re-election of the Labour LCC administration in 1937 with a greatly increased majority. The ideals it embodied served as a model for much of the war-time and post-war reconstruction of the social security and welfare services.

An Act in 1929 had transferred to the Council all the hospital and medical services provided by the 25 **Boards of Guardians** and the **Metropolitan Asylums Board**, including some 74 hospitals providing over 43,000 beds. (The voluntary hospitals, providing 25% of London's hospital beds remained outside the new system.) Many of the new acquisitions were in an appalling state of repair, with primitive medical and back-up facilities. Maternity and isolation cases in particular were very inadequately provided for. Above all, medical and nursing services were chronically understaffed.

From the start, the Council saw its aim as the provision of a municipal health service providing the full range of services – from the cradle to the grave. Medical services were removed from the traditional Poor Law services into a unified public health administration. The pattern was to be a large local general hospital in each locality with specialist centres serving the whole metropolitan area. Thus; Lambeth Hospital came to specialise in cancer treatment; St James' in Fulham in plastic surgery; rheumatism was treated at St Stephens', while Queen Mary's hospital in Carshalton in Surrey became internationally reknowned for its treatment of handicapped children.

MATERNITY
BENEFIT

SPECS AND TEETH

SORRY – WE
CAN'T DO MUCH
FOR YOU NOW.

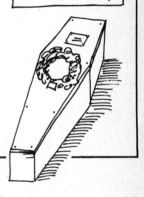

Why does the
LCC give us
milk at school,
Henry? Is it
to stop us
having bandy
legs?

No. It's a common
trick of all prison
institutions, Violet.
They put bromide
in it to reduce our
sex drive!

The capital cost was high. Old hospitals ha[d] to be modernised and new ones built, and back-up laboratory services provided; sinc[e] Poor Law hospitals had not provided out-patient services these had to be established [in] the new general hospitals. To tackle the sta[ff] shortages the Labour administration increased the number of trained nurses by almost 700 with a further extra 400 ward orderlies within a year of taking office. By July 1934, 37 additional doctors were in po[st]

The maternity services underwent the most radical transformation. Poor Law maternity services – such as they were – were widely regarded as an absolute last resort. An emergency domiciliary 'flying squad' and a home midwifery and maternity nursing service were established. Between 1932 and 1937 confinements in LCC hospitals almost doubled, ante-natal attendances in out patient clinics went up from 48,000 to 132,000; as a result the maternal death rate dropped from 7.2 to 2.5 per thousand births.

In the area of mental health the reorganisation of services under one authority opened the way to much-needed improvements. Although the service was predominantly hospital-based, the developing social services worked in tandem with the hospitals. Life in the community became possible for many mental patients.

Fig 55: Measuring a child's head.

The pioneering work in the early days of the LCC in the field of education came under threat in the 1930s as the government cuts in spending began to be felt. Before 1931, government and the LCC contributed equal funds for the education service. After the 1931 **National Economy Act** the government share fell to 37%, forcing the Council to find an extra £1 million a year just to maintain provisions.

Hello. I'm Ramsay MacDonald. I'm famous for being a Labour traitor in the 1931-35 National Government, which I led, and which introduced cuts in workers' living standards.

I would be grateful if you would forget me now. Everyone else has.

Much of the service was in desperate need of rebuilding. 150 elementary schools needed refurbishing or total rebuilding, and all were in need of re-equipping. Many schools were over-crowded, with infant classes averaging over 50 children per teacher, and elementary and central schools at 31. The scholarship system for secondary education deprived thousands of the chance of a decent secondary education.

DOCTOR WALLOP : What is that behind your back, Brown?

BROWN (cleverly): It is an effigy of the Minister of Education, Doctor. We intend to stick pins into it until he pays you a decent salary.

The Council's plans were embodied in its 1935 **Three Year Programme**. The emphasis was on rebuilding. At the same time – within the constraints of the national **Education Acts** – radical changes were made in the examination system, with scholarship examinations broadened, and the number of free places to secondary schools increased to over 50%. Income limits for scholarships were increased, school journeys were more heavily subsidised and grants were provided for uniforms and school meals.

The Council turned its hand to town planning. A city-wide plan was drawn up in consultation with the boroughs, to regulate new building and development. A start was made on a series of road-improvements designed to relieve London's chronic traffic congestion.

In co-operation with the Home Counties the **Green Belt** took shape, with the Council setting aside £2 million towards the cost of buying open spaces to allow London's lungs to breathe. London's parks were transformed, with recreation and sports facilities.

106

Enormously popular free dances were organised in the parks on sunny evenings.

Perhaps the issue which most captured the public's imagination was **Herbert Morrison's** absolute determination to go ahead with the rebuilding of Waterloo Bridge. The rapidly crumbling fabric of the bridge had been patched and shored up by the Tory council in the 1920s and a temporary bridge put up when it became clear that the old one was collapsing. The new Labour Council set their collective hearts on a new bridge – but the capital expenditure was vetoed by the Government.

MORRISON OPENING THE NEW WATERLOO BRIDGE

The project was set in hand anyway. By the time construction work was underway the Government bowed to the inevitable and agreed a 60% grant towards the new bridge, although in a fit of pique they refused any help towards the cost of demolition of the old one.

Herbert Morrison, the leader of the LCC during the crucial years of Labour control in the 1930s, was the original Mr London, and almost the only Labour politican to have risen to the top through local government. His life exactly paralleled the institution he came to symbolise. He was born in 1888, the year the LCC was established, and died in 1965, the year of its demise. He was a formative and life-long influence in the London Labour Party, of which he was the driving force, acting as its secretary and organiser from 1915 during a period of massive growth in power and influence for the party. Mayor of Hackney in 1919, elected to the LCC for East Woolwich in 1922, and MP for South Hackney 1923-4 and 1929-31, he became leader of the LCC following the 1934 Labour victory.

An enormously popular figure in London, he built the London party into an effective machine. His crusading leadership of the LCC provided the most effective opposition to the Tory Government – even though after left-wing beginnings he moved rapidly towards the centre of the Labour Party spectrum as the pragmatic politician *par excellence*.

A highly ambitious politician – good at making enemies from all sides of the party – Morrison failed to get the one job he really wanted – leader of the Labour Party. But he knew how to use the press to get his message home – and deliberately created a public persona which the newspapers loved to caricature: specs, a quiff of hair, baggy suit, always carrying agenda papers and minutes, and hurrying everywhere: the cheerful cockney with a heart of gold.

Morrison? 'E woz wiv "affection beaming in one eye, and calculation shining out of the other."

CHARLES DICKENS – 'MARTIN CHUZZLEWIT'

The Council set in train a progressive employment policy. Direct labour was expanded, the ban on married women teachers and doctors was lifted, pay scales were increased for all council employees, and firms and contractors dealing with the Council were obliged to guarantee fair wages and conditions for their employees.

UNION MEETING — WED. 2·30 pm

DIRECT WORKS DEPT

Don't say "please Miss" Ernie - say "please Ms."

GONE TO LUNCH — Bob Cratchitt

PAY DEMAND

Bloody Council!

None of this was achieved without substantial opposition from the government and its supporters in the media, who constantly forecast that the expansion in public services would 'bankrupt the metropolis'. Like today, the Labour administration believed that increasing public spending on social and welfare provisions would provide more jobs and help revive London's economy. Given that so much expansion was based on capital projects, inevitably the LCC had to undertake a massive borrowing exercise – some of which is still being repaid today. But, on the whole, the strategy paid off. When in 1936 a new stock issue of LCC consolidated stock was made, investors scrambled to acquire it to the extent that it was seventeen times over-subscribed in five minutes. *The Times* commented : 'the finances of the LCC are in a flourishing condition'.

THE POWER OF THE MEDIA

LEFT: "THE EXPANSION OF PUBLIC SERVICES WILL BANKRUPT THE METROPOLIS"

RIGHT: BUT, HELLO - "THE FINANCES OF THE LCC ARE IN A FLOURISHING CONDITION"!

HOW CAN THIS BE?

The LCC criticised the Conservative Government's complete lack of interest in civil defence. The experience of mass bombings in Spain had resulted in the Council laying its own plans by 1937. All Council buildings, for example, had to incorporate structural precautions against air attack. An air raids precautions committee was set up to plan the protection of the city and its people.

NEVILLE CHAMBERLAIN RETURNS FROM HIS MEETING WITH HITLER IN MUNICH – 1939

Evacuation. June 1940

When war did come, the evacuation of the city's children was the first test: over 1.3 million children and mothers with children under five were involved. Half a million children and 20,000 teachers were evacuated smoothly in the first few weeks. Although many subsequently drifted back a further series of evacuations took place as the Nazi bombing campaign intensified. The children, packed into as many clothes as they could wear, clutching suitcases and brown paper parcels, were taken in buses to the major train stations, and decanted into the countryside with little or no idea where they were going or what they would do when they got there.

Crikey – what's that!

Children from the East End did not know what cows were; adults in the reception areas were appalled at the undernourished state of many of the children. Evacuation revealed how much of **Disraeli's** 'two nations' society Britain remained.

The civil defence forces were mustered; the auxiliary fire services, the ambulance and the rescue services, the emergency hospitals organisation. Air raid shelters were built – or taken over, in the case of the London Underground railway.

Despite complaints in some papers about the amount of money being lavished on air raid precautions during the Phoney War, when the bombing did begin on 7 September 1940 the massive effort to defend London's people was quickly proved right.

THE BLITZ

The Pen is Mightier: J J Lynx: LINDSAY DRUMMOND 1946.

Strube

"Is it all right now, Henry?"
"Yes, not even scratched"

Maintaining the fabric of social life during the war also became Council priority. 150 rest centres to cope with people bombed out of their homes were set up, providing food, equipment and nursing attention. More than 250,000 homeless people were admitted to them during the war.

News-Reel. "Tommy's Welcome from pretty French Miss"

much-admired Londoners' meals service was established to feed the homeless and to
provide food for those unable to cook at home because water, electricity or gas supplies had
been cut, or kitchens destroyed. A chain of over 200 cafes was set up serving over 340,000
meals a week, as well as kerbside feeding stations.

The LCC maintained as many of its 'normal'
welfare and education services as possible.
The evacuated children were not forgotten –
LCC officials followed them to the reception
areas, bringing school equipment. Hospital
services were massively stretched by heavy
bomb damage.

Bombing damaged 80,000 homes beyond repair. A further 700,000 suffered damage to some degree – 80% of London's homes. Some areas of the city – the East End, Southwark – had suffered hugely. Dislocation of industry particularly in the docks areas was enormous. The LCC area suffered 49,000 civilian casualties. Restoration and reconstruction was the order of the day.

175
(and more)
DOWN

MORE than 175 German 'planes and at least 350 airmen were shot down in the morning and afternoon attacks on London yesterday.

The R.A.F. lost 30 machines and 20 airmen. In addition, German losses include:

18
on Saturday

Under Labour, government and capital will co-operate!

I'll let them work out what **kind** of capital I'm talking about!

Clement Attlee

If the 1930s had been a time of Labour London versus Conservative Government, the post-war landslide Labour victory seemed to open the way for co-operation between capital and government. After all, several ex-LCC stalwarts were in the Cabinet, among them **Morrison**, and **Lewis Silkin**, the former influential Chair of the LCC **Housing Committee** responsible for slum clearance programme and now Minister for Town and Country Planning. The new Government's commitment to planning as the priority for reconstruction was embodied in the 1947 **Town and Country Planning Act** which confirmed the LCC's role as the planning authority for the County. But the problems of co-ordination with the wider metropolitan area remained.

I suppose Labour's doing it's best, Terry – but I'm not sure I stormed ashore in the first wave at Normandy for the right to live in a pre-fab!

During the 1930s the county boroughs and the county councils had tried to resist LCC purchase of land outside its boundaries for the new housing estates, to keep the slum dwellers at bay and limit LCC influence. As soon as the war ended LCC officials were once again seen to be seizing prime sites, "like the wolf coming down on the fold", as one agitated Tory county councillor remarked.

> If t'LCC buys your farm, I suppose you'll 'ave to go and live with t'pigs, Seth!

The Government plumped for the New Town solution. The 1946 Act set up the **Development Corporations** backed directly by Treasury funds and independent of existing local authorities. By the end of 1949 13 new towns had been designated – eight of them around London. The strategy effectively ended LCC attempts to acquire further housing land outside its boundaries.

BELOW : LIFE IN A NEW TOWN

Before crossing the road at a Zebra Crossing make quite sure that the traffic has stopped.

The LCC's own priorities were set out in the **Abercrombie Plan** published by the end of the war. Apart from welfare and education programmes the Council would direct its energies to the four great defects of London: depressed housing, traffic congestion, the lack of open spaces and the jumble of housing. Communities would be based around neighbourhood units following the lines of well-established community boundaries, with their own schools, social and welfare centres and other amenities.

RIGHT: HOW DAGENHAM WOULD LOOK UNDER THE ABERCROMBIE PLAN

I remember telling the LCC at the time that it was a mistake to put the men's swimming pool so close to the girls' school

The question of population density was to be solved by a pyramidical zoning. The pattern of new housing would be based on a heavy concentration of flats.

Now, there is no doubt that the estates of flats – a pattern subsequently followed by the boroughs – were misconceived. But it is perhaps easy to forget the slums they replaced…

FLATS FLATS FLATS FLATS FL
TS FLATS FLATS FLATS FLATS
FLATS FLATS FLATS FLATSF
FLATS FLATS FLATS LONEL
INESS FLATS FLATS FLATSF
LATS FLATS FLATS FLATSFL
ATS FLATS ISOLATION FLAT
S FLATS FLATS FLATS FLATS
FLATS FLATS FLATS FLATS
FLATS FLATS FLATS FLATS
FLATS FLATS DESPERATI
ON FLATS FLATS FLATS FL
ATS FLATS FLATS FLATS FL
ATS FLATS FLATS FLATSF
LATS FLATS FLATS FLATSF
LATS DEPRESSION FLAT
SFLATS FLATS FLATS FLA
TS FLATS FLATS FLATS F
LATS INTERMINABLE DUL
L TELEVISION PROGRAM
MES FLATS FLATS FLATS
FLATS FLATS FLATS FLAT
SFLATS FLATS MORE FL
ATS FLATS FLATS FLAT
FLATS FLATS FLATS FLAT
SFLATS FLATS PISS IN T
HE LIFT FLATS FLATS
FLATS FLATS FLATS FL
ATS FLATS FLATS FLAT
SFLATS NO PETS FLAT
SFLATS FLATS FLATS F
LATS FLATS FLATS FL
ATS FLATS FLATS FLA
TS FLATS FLATS MORE
BLOODY FLATS FLATS F
LATS FLATS FLATS FLA
TS FLATS FLATS FLAT
SFLATS FL ATS F

VALIUM

122

hroughout the 1950s the LCC remained under Labour control. Meanwhile the Conservative overnment was coming under increasing pressure from its supporters in London local overnment to do something about it. By 1952 a Tory front organisation, the **London Municipal Society**, under its director **Enoch Powell** was calling for the abolition of the LCC.

Abolish the LCC!

Jaturally the Government did not share the LCC's priorities. In 1955 it vetoed large sections f the LCC's development plan which would have increased council housing in its own uburbs. Private enterprise should take the initiative (and the working classes would be kept ut of desirable areas). Instead the LCC should concentrate on housing development in the cruffier inner city sites, near to railways and industry.

Good news children — the government's going to rehouse us near the asbestos works!

The boroughs within the LCC area – both Labour and Tory – wanted more power. This pressure coincided with the increasing need to plan London as a whole. A succession of planned new boundaries for greater London planning were discussed. They were either jettisoned or ignored – at the same time as London's boundaries were growing even to the outskirts of the new towns closest to the metropolis.

LONDON going out of Town — or

The March of Bricks & Mortar !

George Cruikshank

125

Jobs remained concentrated in the centre of the city. Transport for commuters had become a nightmare. By 1951 a quarter of the people in the outer belt, places like Orpington and Sidcup, were travelling into central London each day to work.

ORPINGTON

At last, the Tory Government in 1957 set up a Royal Commission on London government – the **Herbert Commission**.

Will Herbert make life better for commuters?

I hope so. I'm Herbert!

126

The pressure to abolish the LCC came from the Conservative Party and its desire to gain control over London by incorporating the London suburbs into a wider **Greater London**. Documents from Conservative Central Office show that it was from here that the political decision was taken to create a metropolitan authority for London in expectation of Conservative control. For the Tories were forced to recognise the sinister popularity of the LCC among Londoners: their new LCC leader argued that any frontal attack would be exploited by Labour during the 1958 LCC elections. One Tory solution was a wider authority – but one nominated by boroughs – a Metropolitan Board of Works on a grand scale.

Conservative Central Office debating the LCC's future

127

The Herbert Commission was tied by the terms of its brief. It was set up only to consider the organisation of functions actually being performed already by London local authorities. As a result the bureaucratic **Metropolitan Water Board**, the **Port of London Authority** and the **London Passenger Transport Board** remained untouched, as did the separately-managed health authorities in London.

A TYPICAL BOARD MEETING

The Commission reported: the boroughs were to be the primary deliverers of services like refuse collection, roads, social services education where these could most effective be done locally. A new **Greater London Council** would be the strategic authority for the whole metropolitan area, responsible fo looking at the overall needs of the city, and providing those services which cut across borough boundaries.

Hello - look what Herbert's thrown away!

What's this new GLC all about, Albert?

It's a ploy by the Tories to get rid of the LCC - which has usually been controlled by Labour, Alf.

Above all, the Commission insisted that the new GLC would be directly elected. To ensure that its members would see themselves as responsible for London as a whole, their constituencies would not follow borough lines but would be the same as the constituency boundaries which elected MPs to Parliament.

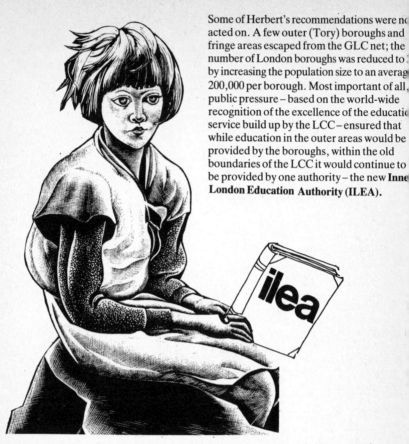

Some of Herbert's recommendations were no acted on. A few outer (Tory) boroughs and fringe areas escaped from the GLC net; the number of London boroughs was reduced to by increasing the population size to an averag 200,000 per borough. Most important of all public pressure – based on the world-wide recognition of the excellence of the education service build up by the LCC – ensured that while education in the outer areas would be provided by the boroughs, within the old boundaries of the LCC it would continue to be provided by one authority – the new **Inner London Education Authority (ILEA).**

The new structure which became law in the 1963 **London Government Act** had one entirely unforeseen consequence. Labour won the first election to the GLC in 1964.

Next time we try to fiddle the voting boundaries I'll ask them how they do it in Northern Ireland!

The Labour Party had been vociferous in its condemnation of the abolition of the LCC. It regarded the new enlarged GLC as an outright gerrymander designed simply to ensure Tory rule in London. But, confounding both Tory and Labour, the new GLC soon showed signs of continuing with the policies of the old LCC – but over a much wider area. Had Tory plans backfired? The GLC continued to build public housing – particularly after an exceptionally nasty slum housing scandal in August 1963 – the **Rachman** affair – laid bare the activities of private landlords and speculators in terrorising London's poorest citizens.

It's Mr Rachman for the rent, dear!

REFORMISM

Indeed, the new GLC now had the power to extend public housing into the old leafy suburbs – and it did, with the backing of the new Labour Government under **Harold Wilson** elected in 1964.

HAROLD WILSON

A week is a long time in politics – but normal length when you go up to the House of Lords, like me.

Why d'you call your cat 'Horace'?

When the Tories won control of the GLC in 1967, public hostility to the plans of the Tory GLC housing chairman **Horace Cutler** to end public housing by the GLC was enormous.

He's got whiskers and we want to put him out a lot!

Throughout the 1960s housing remained the major political issue in London as a succession of reports and exposés in the newspapers revealed the scale of the housing crisis. It was an issue which caught the Tories full in the face, with their insistence on the role of private builders and their hostility to the needs of council tenants and people with low incomes at high housing need.

By 1973, when Labour defeated the Tories in that year's GLC elections, planning and roads in London were hitting the headlines. The Tory GLC leader, **Desmond Plummer**, was an inveterate developer. His plans to enclose London within a motorway box, with the devastation of vast areas of housing to allow for new dual carriageways cutting across London caused an uproar. Londoners breathed a collective sigh of relief when the plans were dropped after the Labour victory.

Equally controversial was Plummer's vision of large scale office development in the heart of the city – symbolised by the monstrous **Centre Point** tower block at the junction of Oxford Street and Tottenham Court Road which has remained largely unoccupied since its construction.

The Tories' determination to limit the role of the GLC in providing services and meeting need reached its height in the **Cutler** years of 1977-81, following a Conservative (Tory) victory in 1977. **Sir Horace** – a showman with a florid style reminiscent of the Victorian music hall – decided: GLC houses would be sold by lottery, complete with a spinning wheel of fortune; London's derelict dockland would be the site of the 1984 Olympic Games; London would become a free trade area.

SIR HORACE CUTLER

135

The GLC's services rapidly declined, particularly after Cutler finally achieved the long term Tory dream and transferred the bulk of the GLC's housing stock to the boroughs. The full effects of the British economic recession hit the capital – but the Tories stood by and did nothing. By 1981 over 200,000 of London's workers were out of a job – and in some parts of London unemployment was double the national average.

Unemployed Londoner: "Bless yer, kind lady! I'm that 'ungry I got to eat grass."

Dear Old Lady: "If you go round to the back you'll find the grass grows much longer and thicker there."

The Labour Party in London saw its opportunity. The party's 1981 GLC election manifesto promised as a priority that the long-term deterioration in **London Transport** (transferred to the GLC in 1969) with its spiral of hugely increased fares, falling passenger numbers, decline of bus and tube services and deteriorating stock would be halted. Industrial decline would be challenged by the establishment of a **Greater London Enterprise Board** with the funds to save jobs in firms damaged by the recession, and build up the new industries. Londoners, particularly those in minority groups, and those whose interests had traditionally been ignored or under-represented in local government, like women and ethnic minorities, would be brought into the political process. London's vast range of voluntary organisations would be better funded. The GLC's housing role would be revived, with more homes built and renovated.

Special priority would be given for those in need: the single homeless, the elderly, ethnic minorities.

On the planning side, priority would be given to building up home and community facilities. Office sprawl would be halted.

On this radical socialist manifesto – and in the teeth of unprecedented press hostility – the Labour Party won a majority of four on 7th May 1981. The wheel had come full circle. London's local government would once again be fighting for the capital's interests against hostile government. The curtain had opened on a four-year political drama that would change the face and image of local government for ever.

Within hours of Labour's victory, the scene was set by the media. When **Ken Livingstone** beat **Andrew MacKintosh** for the job of Labour Leader – and thereby Leader of the Council – Fleet Street decided it was all an extreme socialist plot, and a threat to civilisation as we know it. This was despite the fact that Livingstone won by a wide margin of ten votes in the GLC's **Labour Group**, where the left were by no means always assured of a majority.

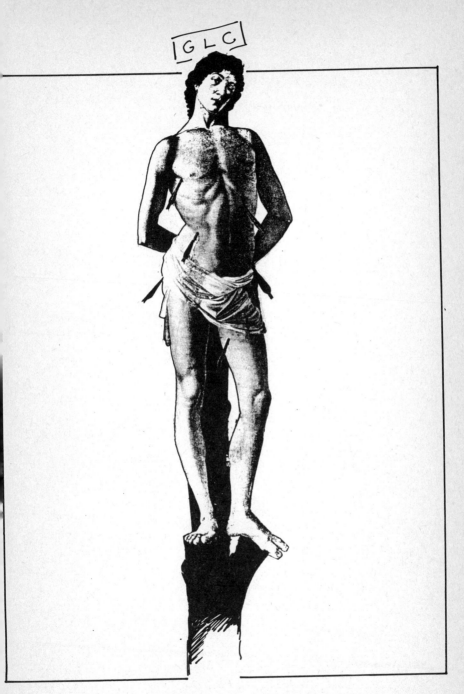

ABOVE: KEN LIVINGSTONE PREPARES TO ACCEPT CRITICISM

The battle over **London Transport** was the first act in the unfolding drama. As a first step to reversing the long term decline of LT, the Labour group was pledged to cut fares and increase the frequency of bus and tube journeys, all of which involved an initial increase in the GLC's subsidy to LT.

The cost of bringing in the policy had been estimated at about £100 million during 1981–82, involving the levying of a supplementary rate of 5p, spelt out in Labour's manifesto. But the Government's massive cuts in rate support grant to local authorities in 1981 meant that any increased subsidy would involve higher supplementary rates of 11.9p – equalling £1.31 a week for the average London rate-payer.

In July, Bromley Council decided to challenge the policy in the courts. Long the implacable foes of any progressive policy – particularly if it emanated from the GLC – and the bastion of right wing Conservatism – Bromley maintained that the increased rate and the subsidy to London Transport was unreasonable, even though a policy of subsidy had been expressly included in the 1969 Transport (London) Act. Although Bromley lost the case in the Divisional Court they proceeded to appeal – and in a sensational reversal of established wisdom, the Appeal Court, on November 1981, declared the fares cut and the supplementary rate illegal.

There is no doubt that the judges' interpretation – that the GLC had no right to run LT at a deficit subsidy even if this was in the interests of Londoners – was influenced by the political climate of the time; the hysterical press attacks on Livingstone, and the Government's clampdown on local authority spending. If, however, they expected the grateful thanks of an over-rated populace, the judges were wrong. What particularly incensed London opinion were the inflammatory political comments which accompanied the judgement. **Lord Denning** in particular threw scorn on manifesto commitments: 'many electors did not vote for the manifesto, they voted for the party. When a party was returned to power, it should consider what it was best to do, and what was practical and fair.' The **House of Lords** upheld the Appeal Court decision: the GLC had abandoned 'business principles' in the *Fares Fair* policy, said **Lord Scarman**. It was a breach of duty to the ratepayers, said Lord **Diplock**.

The effect of the judgement was clear. Fares would have to increase by 300% and concessions like free travel for old age pensioners halted. Not surprisingly, the GLC policy began to attract widespread support, even from the media, and around London meetings held to support *Fares Fair* attracted some of the largest crowds for years. But the Labour administration did not give up. Although fares did increase in 1982 as the Council reluctantly complied with the Lords ruling, by 1983 a new package was ready: it cut the fares again by 25%, introduced a new zoning system that made travelling short distances cheaper, introduced the travel card, which made using buses and tubes an attractive prospect. Free travel opportunities for pensioners and the disabled were increased. The results of the 1983 *Just the Ticket* package of the travelcard and the 25% fares reduction were spectacular. London Transport gained an extra £48 million in revenue from fares, with a 16% increase in the use of LT's services – equivalent to an extra 300 journey miles a year. The number of cars travelling into central London went down by 10% in one year.

Note: the 'Conqueror' sank the Argentine 'Belgrano' during the Falklands (Malvinas) War. 300 died.

The Labour manifesto's commitment to turn round the decline in London's economy was also tackled. The **Greater London Enterprise Board** was set up as the cornerstone of the new industrial strategy. By 1983 the overall budget for the programme was £110 million.

The plight of London's growing unemployed was highlighted by a massive sign on the roof of County Hall facing Parliament displaying the monthly unemployment statistics.

At last we've got a lovely GLC council house, Eric – and if you've ruptured yourself there's a very good community hospital!

On the housing side, the Labour group developed the largest housing programme in the country, tackling renovations and repairs for around 200,000 homes, and managing the 74,000 homes still under GLC ownership. It developed a mobility scheme for council tenants, to enable them to move across borough boundaries where needed.

It provided special facilities for those in extreme need – dossers; alcoholics; ex-offenders and the mentally ill.

The emphasis was put on building homes and community facilities rather than on offices. Hundreds of London's acres were saved from the developers' bulldozers. Sites like Coin Street on the South Bank have been saved.

Tory cuts in many areas were reversed. The Fire Brigade was brought back to strength with new fire appliances.

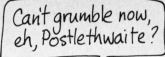

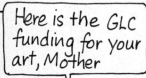

Funding for the arts and cultural centres was increased, particularly outside the traditional "centres of excellence". By 1983 the GLC was investing over £7.25 million in the arts across London, and supporting dozens of sports facilities, including the **National Sports Centre** at Crystal Palace.

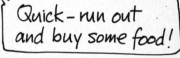

The GLC attacked the Government's ludicrous plans for civil defence.

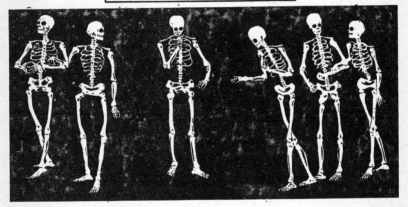

The danger to London from nuclear waste transportation was exposed. London was declared a 'nuclear free zone'. This move was quickly adopted elsewhere.

Work on the massive London flood defences, including the **Thames Barrier** across the Thames at Woolwich Reach, was stepped up.

I declare this dam open!

Watch your language your majesty – the media are watching!

THAMES BARRIER

← Our Ken.

It was the Labour-controlled Council's policies for tackling the denial of equal opportunities for women, and ethnic minority groups which most enraged the Tories across the water, in Parliament.

PRIVILEGE

LADIES

Racism, and discrimination against women, was tackled head on – in the Council's own employment policies, in the policies of firms and companies trading with the GLC, in the policies of the Council's own services such as the arts and housing.
For example, when the Labour GLC first took over there were seven black and no women firefighters in London. By 1984 these figures had increased to 50 and eight.
The interests of gay men and lesbian women were similarly taken up.

The impact of government cuts in statutory services led to a great flowering of voluntary services across London. Labour greatly increased funding to these groups: by 1984 over 2,000 London-wide and borough based groups were receiving funds. The vast majority of these were completely non-controversial – **Age Concern**, **MENCAP**, the **Greater London Association for Disabled People**, adoption agencies, citizens advice bureaux… But the Labour Group took the view that minority groups with realistic projects also deserved support. A handful of grants to minority and community groups with something new to say roused the press to extravagant reporting.

AND—THE LOCALS FIGHT BACK. BULLETINS OPPOSE TORY PLANS FOR SOUTH BANK HOTELS AND OFFICES...

The wildest allegations, that the GLC supported international terrorism; that it handed over money to 'lefty loonies'; were made daily. Yet – put together – all the 'controversial' GLC spending amounted to no more than 0.6% of the total GLC budget each year…

In fact, like any large bureaucracy, the GLC can be quite ruthless at times – as with this vegetarian cafe in Islington. In the event the shop was reprieved, but the Council has proved many times that it can be a hard landlord and a mean employer…

You can say that again!

GLC to force Gipsies out

HAMPSTEAD AND HIGHGATE EXPRESS 6:7:1984

≥ HOWEVER... ≥

...y of the innovations were enormous successes.
...4, for example, was nominated as the GLC's
...-**Racist Year**. A host of community events and
...ivals, conferences and discussions involved about
...ethnic minority communities in London.

BILL MAULDIN 1962

You ain't gaining too much altitude holding me down!

153

The redevelopment of London's docklands – the symbol of the capital's economic decline – illustrates the growing conflict between local authority and central government views of planning and development. A rapid programme of dock closures began in the late 1960s when St Katherine's docks closed, to be followed by a succession of upstream enclosed docks. The last ship – a Soviet timber ship – sailed from the famous Surrey docks in 1970, leaving the entire area largely derelict. The GLC and the five London boroughs concerned set up the docklands joint committee in 1973, following a joint government-GLC study.

The joint committee af extensive local consultation produced the **London Docklands Strategic Plan** in 1976, which set out a programme of development that woul preserve local communities and such industry as remained, while allowing redevelopment for new industries. Such integrated community planning proved anathema to the incom Tory Government of 1979. Rejecting the LDSP, they moved swiftly to take all planning control away from the local authoriti concerned in 1980 and s up instead an unaccountable quango the **London Docklands Development Corporation** – and designated the Isle of Dogs an 'Enterprise Zone'.

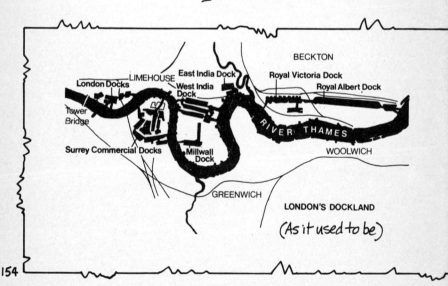

LONDON'S DOCKLAND

(As it used to be)

In contrast, the Covent Garden redevelopment by the GLC has proved a remarkable success story. When the fruit and flower market moved to its new site south of the Thames in Battersea the GLC moved quickly to ensure that the vacant site was not simply handed over to office developers. Instead the entire area was to be restored to something approaching **Inigo Jones**' original conception, with the central market place area revitalised by shops and workshops.

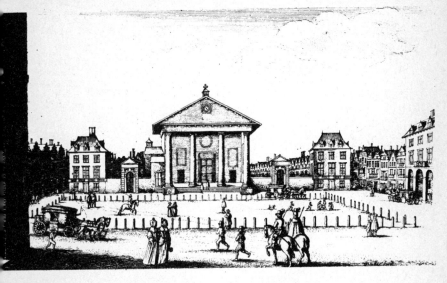

Despite some initial County Hall skirmishes between Tories anxious to allow as much untrammelled private development as possible, and the Labour Group determined to maintain a balanced redevelopment, the final project has proven an enormous success, both as an oasis of shops and restaurants, a meeting place for Londoners and as a tourist attraction. The Covent Garden project is continuously cited around the world as the type of development which retains the original character of a site of historic importance, while retaining its local community and economic viability.

ONE-MAN
COVENT
GARDEN
OPEN-AIR
OPERA.
TODAY—
'THE RING'

The Thatcher Government had already tried to defeat the new style GLC. As part of its programme of cuts in local authority spending – and as a deliberate measure to bring the GLC to heel – a system of cuts in government grants to local authorities was devised, based on a penalty system when the authority spent above an arbitrary government target figure for spending and services.

By 1983 the GLC had lost £1,200 million in Government grant – and was receiving no block grant at all.
As a direct consequence the rate levied by the GLC was increased between 1981 and 1983 by 118% – half of which was due directly to the loss of grant.

The Tory Government then moved directly against the Council. The press coverage of events at County Hall and the rate increases had, **Margaret Thatcher** felt, created the atmosphere in which a pledge to abolish the GLC outright would be a positive vote winner. It would also direct attention away from the Government's failure to implement its 1979 election manifesto commitment to abolish domestic rates. Despite all the advice from Tory Cabinet Ministers with local government experience, from **Michael Heseltine** to **Tom King**, that the GLC abolition was just not a practical proposition, **Thatcher** personally inserted into the Tory 1983 election manifesto the following immortal words:

The metropolitan councils and the GLC have been shown to be a wasteful and unnecessary tier of government. We shall abolish them and return most of their functions to the boroughs and districts.

Services... such as the Police and fire service and education... will be run by joint boards...

The metropolitan county councils, Tyne and Wear, South and West Yorkshire, Merseyside, Greater Manchester, West Midlands, directly elected like the GLC, were tacked into the commitment as an afterthought. No-one had ever seriously considered abolishing them, but they did serve to camouflage what was an outright assault on one council – the GLC

Abolition of the GLC, as proposed by the Thatcher Government, turns the clock back on one hundred years of local government development. As we shall see, it proposes to do away entirely with a city-wide administration. Instead, above borough level, will be a plethora of appointed, unelected and unaccountable joint boards and quangoes – uncannily reminiscent of the mess that existed before the LCC.

What's a 'Quango', Vera?

A Quango is a Quasi-Autonomous Non-Governmental Organisation, Dorothy, responsible to no-one.

Unlike previous re-organisations all this is to be rushed through without a Royal Commission or enquiry, and without public debate.

The only recent public enquiry into the GLC – the 1978 **Marshall Enquiry** carried out at the behest of **Horace Cutler** – found firmly in favour of retaining the GLC as the London–wide authority. Its author was **Sir Frank Marshall**, now national Vice-President of the Conservative Party. One submission to Marshall from a London Tory MP read: "I believe we must now return to the concept of the GLC as the strategic authority for London". The London MP concerned was **Patrick Jenkin**, now the Secretary of State for the Environment, who has responsibility for carrying out the abolition plans.

this book goes to press, the battle over abolition is in full swing. But it is already clear that –
e the other great Tory attempt to restructure London's government to suit party purpose –
e plan has backfired. Far from being a vote-winner, the plan to abolish the GLC has turned
:o an electoral disaster for the Tories. A series of independent opinion polls has shown that
pport for keeping the Council is as high as 70%. A poll in Thatcher's own Finchley
nstituency showed 66% in favour of the GLC. In the Euro-elections in June 1984, the
ing to Labour in London was twice the national average, and the party gained three seats.

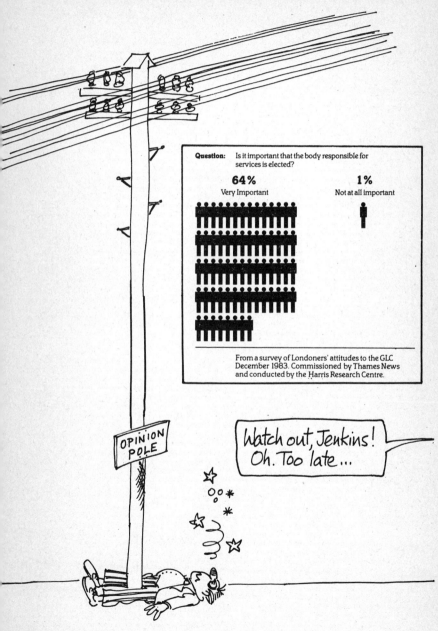

Question: Is it important that the body responsible for services is elected?

64% Very Important

1% Not at all important

From a survey of Londoners' attitudes to the GLC December 1983. Commissioned by Thames News and conducted by the Harris Research Centre.

The Tory plan to abolish the GLC had a fatal flaw. It was clear that even without an official enquiry and with the legislation rushed through Parliament on the back of the Government's huge majority, abolition would take at least two years. But the elections for the GLC and the metropolitan councils fell due in May 1985. The Government decided to rush a Bill through Parliament to cancel the elections, and to substitute a body consisting of 'nominated' borough councillors to run the councils for the interim period until abolition. In London, this would have the effect of transferring power from an elected Labour authority to an unelected Tory one – without a single vote being cast. This was described by former Tory Prime Minister **Edward Heath** as

-the greatest piece of gerrymandering over the last 150 years!

He was only one of a number of senior Tory figures who opposed the measure.

The GLC issue was seized on by the **House of Lords**. With an eye to their own long-term survival – but perhaps also a genuine concern to fulfill their supposed role as defenders of the constitution – their noble Lords and Ladyships inflicted the most significant political defeat of its five years in office on the Government. On 28 June, and by the massive margin of 48 votes, the Upper House unceremoniously threw out the Government's plan to institute a nominated authority after May 1985. The so-called 'Paving Bill' was denounced on all sides as unconstitutional.

R. DOYLE. Hyghest Court of Law in ye Kingdom.
Ye Lords hearing Appeals. 1849.

This unprecedented defeat threw the Government into turmoil – cruelly exposed the utter inadequacy of their proposals. After several weeks of hurried consultations with the recalcitrant Tory peers and cross-bench Lords who had been outraged by the proposals – the Government came up with a compromise. Even though the Lords' vote had been clearly designed to enable the 1985 elections to go ahead, the Government remained determined at all costs to avoid such an election since it would clearly turn into a popular referendum on the abolition itself – with the utterly certain prospect of a massive defeat at the polls for the Tory candidates.

Nor was the irony of an unelected institution – the Lords – coming to the rescue of an elected GLC, and a left wing administration like that of Ken Livingstone – wasted.

Is–is that you, Denis?

Why did you vote against the abolition of the GLC, Lord Mental-Case?

Becorse I thought one good turn might desarve another!

Instead – and although **Mrs Thatcher** herself had previously proclaimed in the Commons that such a course would not be countenanced – the Government decided to extend the terms of office of the incumbent Labour administration for a year, until abolition in April 1986. Although the plan was rejected by the Labour Party both at the GLC and in Parliament the Government mustered sufficient support for it, and the amended **Paving Bill** received its Royal Assent on 31 July 1984.

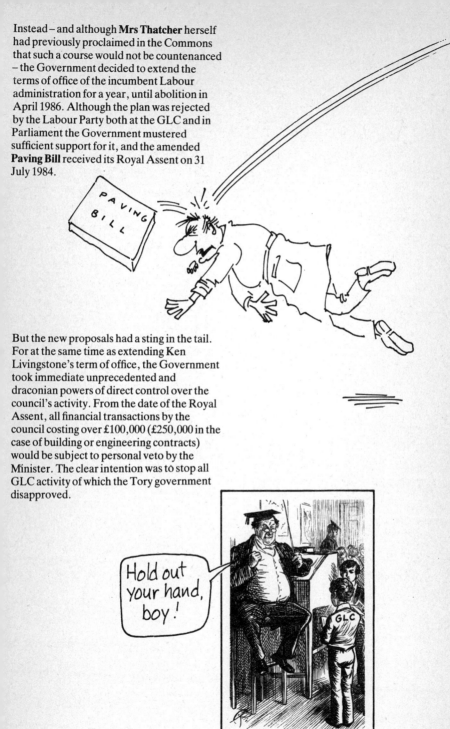

But the new proposals had a sting in the tail. For at the same time as extending Ken Livingstone's term of office, the Government took immediate unprecedented and draconian powers of direct control over the council's activity. From the date of the Royal Assent, all financial transactions by the council costing over £100,000 (£250,000 in the case of building or engineering contracts) would be subject to personal veto by the Minister. The clear intention was to stop all GLC activity of which the Tory government disapproved.

But even with the financial controls – which will produce such absurdities as the GLC requiring Ministerial consent to the purchase of baked beans for London's schools – the Government was unable to disguise the massive defeat it had suffered.

Almost to a person, the media turned on the hapless **Patrick Jenkin** as the man responsible for the Government's humiliation.

ABOVE: JENKIN ACCEPTS THE BLAME.

All the quangoes will of course meet in private, reducing the public and the media's access to information. Above all, their members will be subject only their political paymaster, the Secretary of State, completely unaccountable to the people whose interests they are supposed to serve.

The White Paper does not even mention the GLC's vital work for ethnic minorities and women. The boroughs will be expected to take over support for industry and employment initiatives, and funding voluntary organisations.

All of this is at a time when a combination of vicious cuts in government grant and the threat of rate capping leaves boroughs denuded of funds even to maintain existing statutory services. Not one borough has expressed confidence in being able to take over the full range of GLC services.

London Transport – the GLC's greatest success story – was taken away from the GLC under the 1984 **London Regional Transport Act** in July 1984. A reduced service will be run by the Secretary of State for Transport, and a nominated board, called **London Regional Transport**. Fares will rise and services will be cut to reduce the level of subsidy; profitable sections of the service will be privatised.

TRANSPORT

ENERGY

EDUCATION

ROADS

PRIVATISATION

The argument that the GLC is wasteful and that substantial savings will accrue from abolition does not stand up. Not since the White Paper of 1983 was published has the Government said how much it intends to save. But it is perfectly obvious that the host of joint boards and appointed bodies will require their own bureaucracies, and their members will require their perks; car pools; lunch and expense accounts.

In fact, the GLC is remarkably cost effective – between 1978 and 1983, GLC spending rose by 88%; over the same period central Government spending went up by 101%. Yet it is the GLC that is condemned as profligate and irresponsible, and a threat to national economic recovery. Only 16.5% of GLC spending goes on staffing. The figure for the rest of local government is 60%. Since 1975 the GLC has lost almost 12,000 jobs – a 14% reduction in the last 6 years – at a time when the Government's own bureaucracies have proliferated, and its staff increased.

Ministers say the GLC is 'unrepresentative'. Yet turn-out at GLC elections is higher than at borough elections. People exempted from paying rates vote at local elections – but people vote in national elections who don't pay tax. *Are we to return to the days of the property qualification for the right to vote?*

If the Government's stated arguments in support of abolition don't stand up to scrutiny why is the Government proceeding with its plans, against such a weight of opinion and advice? *The answer lies with* **Margaret Thatcher** *and her style of government.* She gave the commitment – and she will not back down.

This Government cannot tolerate opposition in any form – and particularly legitimate democratic opposition. *Because* the GLC has come to represent another point of view of how the country can be run, *because* its policies embody much of the alternative strategies of the Labour Party and the trade unions, and above all *because* it is getting increasing support from London's electors, it is a threat to Tory supremacy. It must go.

And in the final analysis it comes down to what Norman Tebbit said in March 1984:

The GLC is typical of this new divisive form of socialism ... so we shall abolish the GLC!

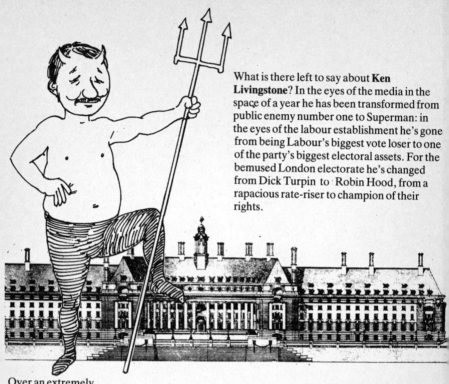

What is there left to say about **Ken Livingstone**? In the eyes of the media in the space of a year he has been transformed from public enemy number one to Superman: in the eyes of the labour establishment he's gone from being Labour's biggest vote loser to one of the party's biggest electoral assets. For the bemused London electorate he's changed from Dick Turpin to Robin Hood, from a rapacious rate-riser to champion of their rights.

Over an extremely difficult three years Livingstone held together a Labour group which spanned the political spectrum, and ensured that radical policies were put into practice by a group on which the left was by no means sure of a majority. Like **Morrison**, a native of South of London, he knows better than almost any other politician around how to use the establishment and the media's own weapons and arguments against them. Above all, he has changed the image of local government from boring committees to fun. Whether local government will ever recover from the shock remains to be seen.

170

The GLC, as we have seen, is not a perfect institution.

But it *is* democratic, subject to control by Londoners who can and do sack administrations they don't like every four years. It holds its meetings in public, and its myriad papers are available for the public and the media. Inconvenient as councillors and officers sometimes find this – it is as it should be, because access to information and accountability are the cornerstones of democracy. Ideally, to be an effective authority, this elected body should control the other London-wide services: water, health, and the metropolitan police.

Who has won the GLC election, Mother?

We have all won, child – because there **is** an election!

But abolition of the GLC will be a triumph for the old vested interests, for private and party interests against public good, for all those who through the years have tried to hold back progress, to prevent London's wealth and services being used for the benefits of all its people. For the people of London's sake, let's hope their triumph will be short-lived.

THE END

As this book goes to press the campaign to save the GLC is in full swing – and there's a wide range of things readers (and writers) can do to help.

● write to your MP stating your view – go and see him/her at their surgery, particularly if they are pro-abolition.

● get any organisation or association you belong to to lobby MPs or Peers.

● if you belong to a project or scheme locally or if you work for an organisation likely to be affected by abolition get them to make their views known publicly.

● join your local *Save the GLC* campaign. You can get your local contact by phoning the campaign line on 01–633 4400.

● display the *Save the GLC* publicity material and get your friends, neighbours and relatives to do the same.

● write to your local paper giving your views.

● contact the GLC on the hotline number 01–633 4400 for information packs on abolition.

● raise the issue in your trade union branch. Make sure your branch plays a leading role in the campaign.

● discuss it in your workplace. Get your co-workers to support stoppages to back the campaign, and go on demonstrations with your workplace name on banners and placards.

BIBLIOGRAPHY

LABOUR IN LONDON - A STUDY IN MUNICIPAL ACHIEVEMENT
    Brian Barker - Routledge 1946

LIFE AND LABOUR OF THE PEOPLE IN LONDON
    Charles Booth (Editor) 1902-3

VICTORIAN CITIES
    Asa Briggs - Odhams 1967

CITIZEN KEN
    John Carvel - Chatto + Windus 1984

LONDON, THE BIOGRAPHY OF A CITY
    Christopher Hibbert - Penguin 1980

THE CITY IN HISTORY
    Lewis Mumford - Secker + Warburg 1961

LONDON : THE CITIES OF LONDON AND WESTMINSTER
    Nikolaus Pevsner - Penguin Revised Edn. 1962

LONDON IN ROMAN TIMES
    Wheeler - London Museum Cats. No. 3 1930

METROPOLITAN LONDON : POLITICS AND URBAN CHANGE 1837-1981
    Ken Young and Patricia Garside - Edward Arnold 1982

LONDON : A PICTORIAL HISTORY
    John Hayes - BT Batsford 1969

THE LABOUR PARTY
    Peter Lane - Batsford 1973

LONDON GROWING
    Michael Harrison - Hutchinson 1965

LONDON : 2000 YEARS OF A CITY AND ITS PEOPLE
    Felix Barker and Peter Jackson - Papermac 1984

THE PEOPLE'S GUIDE TO LONDON
    Andrew Davies - Journeyman 1984

FLY A FLAG FOR POPLAR
    Geoff Richman - Liberation Films

WALKS IN LONDON
    William Kent - Staples Press 1951

LONDON'S RIVER
    Eric de Mare - Bodley Head 1964

STOP PRESS

As we go to press (September 20th 1984) the results of four London GLC by-elections come in. The elections were caused by the resignation of Labour councillors - one of whom was Ken Livingstone - in order to test Londoners' opinion of Thatcher's plan to abolish the GLC. The Conservatives, fearing humiliation, refused to stand. Labour won all four seats - Paddington, Edmonton, Hayes and Harlington and Lewisham - comfortably, with greatly increased majorities.